For my Moon, Sun & Star

"*The only way to have a friend is to be one.*"
— Ralph Waldo Emerson

What's Over That Hill?

A journey of two curious little birds

by Leslie Mullins

What's over that hill?
The two little birds asked.
Blue as far as you can see said their friend Bird.

Be careful though, they say a monster
lives there with big ears, a giant tail,
and long legs to jump at the moon.

The two little birds flew over the hill
and saw a deep blue ocean. They found
no monster only a new friend, Rabbit.

What's over that hill? The two little birds asked.
Orange as far as you can see.

Be careful though, they say a monster
lives there with big eyes, a giant nose,
and sharp teeth to eat up the moon.

The two little birds flew over the hill
and saw a big orange desert. They found
no monster only a new friend, Coyote.

What's over that hill? The two little birds asked.
Green as far as you can see.

Be careful though, they say a monster lives there with big claws, a giant beak, and wide wings to hide the moon.

The two little birds flew over the hill
and saw a giant green forest. They found
no monster only a new friend, Owl.

What's over that hill? The two little birds asked.
White as far as you can see.

Be careful though, they say a monster
lives there with big hooves, a giant head,
and massive horns to shove at the moon.

The two little birds flew over the hill
and saw a mighty white glacier. They found
no monster only a new friend, Ram.

What's over that hill? The two little birds asked.
Silver as far as you can see.

21

Be careful though, they say a monster
lives there with big paws, a giant nose,
and sharp claws to swipe at the moon.

The two little birds flew over the hill
and saw a great silver bay. They found
no monster only a new friend, Bear.

What's over that hill? The two little birds asked.
Gold as far as you can see.

Be careful though, they say a monster lives there with big horns, a giant neck, and strong back to carry away the moon.

The two little birds flew over the hill
and saw an endless golden prairie. They found
no monster only a new friend, Buffalo.

What's over that hill? The two little birds asked.
Blue as far as you can see.

Be careful though, they say a monster
lives there with big wings, giant feet,
and sharp beak to peck at the moon.

The two little birds flew over the hill to find a deep blue ocean. They found no monster only their old friend, Bird.

What's over that hill? Their friend asked.

Friends as far as you can see!

A portion of all royalties donated for the
preservation of our National Parks through
nationalparks.org

www.ingramcontent.com/pod-product-compliance
Lightning Source LLC
Chambersburg PA
CBHW040404100426

42811CB00017B/1830